MAYER SMITH

The Eternal Court of Frost and Flame

Copyright © 2025 by Mayer Smith

All rights reserved. No part of this publication may be reproduced, stored or transmitted in any form or by any means, electronic, mechanical, photocopying, recording, scanning, or otherwise without written permission from the publisher. It is illegal to copy this book, post it to a website, or distribute it by any other means without permission.

This novel is entirely a work of fiction. The names, characters and incidents portrayed in it are the work of the author's imagination. Any resemblance to actual persons, living or dead, events or localities is entirely coincidental.

Mayer Smith asserts the moral right to be identified as the author of this work.

Mayer Smith has no responsibility for the persistence or accuracy of URLs for external or third-party Internet Websites referred to in this publication and does not guarantee that any content on such Websites is, or will remain, accurate or appropriate.

Designations used by companies to distinguish their products are often claimed as trademarks. All brand names and product names used in this book and on its cover are trade names, service marks, trademarks and registered trademarks of their respective owners. The publishers and the book are not associated with any product or vendor mentioned in this book. None of the companies referenced within the book have endorsed the book.

First edition

This book was professionally typeset on Reedsy. Find out more at reedsy.com

Contents

1	The Ashen Arrival	1
2	Flames in the Snow	7
3	The Shattered Mirror	13
4	Beneath the Cinders	20
5	Cold Hands, Warm Heart	26
6	The Inferno's Song	33
7	A Kiss of Flame	39
8	Echoes of the Past	45
9	The Phoenix's Flame	51
10	The Icebound Secret	58
11	The Awakening Flame	65
12	The Burning Veil	72
13	The Ashes of Betrayal	78
14	The Flame and the Frost	84
15	The Final Ember	91

One

The Ashen Arrival

The gates of the Eternal Court loomed like the mouth of a beast, its iron spikes reaching for the heavens. Isolde, daughter of the Frostlands, stared up at them with a mixture of awe and unease. Her breath crystallized in the biting air, the frosty tendrils of her exhale disappearing into the grey mist that surrounded the court. The winds of the Frostlands had always been bitter, harsh, but this was different—this was something else. A subtle shift in the air, as though the world itself was holding its breath.

Behind her, the chill of her homeland seemed far away. The sounds of the Frostlands, the sharp echo of cracking ice and the distant call of winter birds, faded into the background as she took a step forward. The black stone pathway beneath her feet was a stark contrast to the snow that lay like a thick blanket across the land. As she moved closer to the gates, she could feel the weight of the court pressing down on her.

"This is it," she whispered to herself, her voice barely audible over the eerie silence that hung in the air.

The Frostlands had raised her for this moment, had trained her to be the ice-hearted ruler her people needed. Yet, the sight before her stirred something deep within her—a shiver that had nothing to do with the biting cold. The Court of Flame was nothing like the cold and rigid palace of her ancestors. Here, the heat from the palace walls radiated in waves, stifling the air, wrapping around her like a serpent waiting to strike.

"You must stand firm," she murmured, gripping the hem of her cloak as though it might steady her trembling hands. Her fingers ached from the cold, but her mind was a blaze of confusion. What if the Fire King, Ryker, did not want her allegiance? What if he had some hidden agenda that would leave her people defenseless?

The gates creaked open with an unsettling groan, and a figure emerged from the shadows beyond.

Isolde's breath caught in her throat.

A man stood before her—tall, his features sharp like the flames that flickered around him. His eyes, molten amber, burned into her soul, sending a flicker of warmth through her veins. His hair, the color of dark embers, hung loosely around his shoulders, and his cloak shimmered with a fiery glow that seemed to flicker with life of its own. His presence was as commanding as it was

The Ashen Arrival

unnerving.

"You are the Princess of Frostlands, Isolde," he said, his voice smooth, yet laced with a power that made her pulse quicken. "Welcome to the Eternal Court."

His words were laden with both politeness and authority, the kind that demanded respect while carefully concealing any trace of threat. She swallowed, forcing her nerves into submission.

"I am," she replied, her voice steady despite the storm of emotion building within her. She had prepared for this moment, rehearsing her words in the solitude of her chambers. But nothing could have prepared her for the fire that danced in his eyes, the undeniable pull that he had on her. "I have come to pledge my allegiance to the Court of Flame."

Ryker's lips curved into a smile, but it didn't reach his eyes. The flames in his gaze flickered as if searching for something within her, and for a moment, Isolde wondered if he knew something she didn't. Something about her that she had yet to discover.

"Come," he said, his tone now warmer, though still with an edge of danger. "You have traveled far, Princess. Let us take you to the heart of the court. There, your journey begins."

Reluctantly, Isolde stepped forward, the weight of the decision pressing on her chest. She had been trained to distrust everything about the Fire King and his court, but there was something in his voice, something in the way he spoke her name that made her heart race.

The gates behind her shut with a final, echoing thud, trapping her inside the court's walls.

As she walked beside him, the heat from his presence seemed to press against her skin, making the air thick and heavy. It wasn't just the warmth that enveloped her; it was the palpable power of the Court of Flame itself. She could feel it—the weight of the court's ancient magic, pulsing in the very stones beneath her feet.

"The court has waited for you," Ryker said, his voice low, almost conspiratorial. "The bond between our kingdoms must be forged, and I'm afraid only you can do it."

His words sent a ripple through her. Was this why she had been summoned here? To be a bridge between the ice and the fire? She had known this moment would come, but she had never imagined it would feel so... suffocating. A cold sweat broke out across her forehead, despite the warmth around her.

They passed courtiers who barely acknowledged her presence, their faces hidden behind masks of politeness. Their eyes, however, tracked her movements with careful, calculating interest. It was as though the entire court was holding its breath, waiting for something to happen, for her to make her move.

The grandeur of the palace was nothing like the simple, austere beauty of the Frostlands. Gold and crimson banners adorned the walls, and the air was thick with the scent of burning incense

The Ashen Arrival

and charred wood. Every corner of the court seemed to pulse with a life of its own. Isolde couldn't shake the feeling that the court was watching her, testing her.

They arrived at the grand hall—a massive chamber filled with towering pillars of obsidian and firelight. The flames from the grand fireplace danced wildly, casting long, shifting shadows that stretched across the floor. The atmosphere was thick with magic, almost suffocating. In the center of the room stood a large, intricately carved throne, its base forged from the very heart of a volcano. The throne seemed alive, pulsing with an energy that made Isolde's pulse quicken.

Ryker moved toward the throne, his cloak flowing behind him like a trail of smoke.

"Sit," he instructed, motioning to a seat beside his. "You will be treated as my equal here, Princess. As the future ruler of both Frost and Flame."

The words were heavy, laden with promise, but also with an undercurrent of danger. Was he truly offering her equality, or was this all part of a greater game? She couldn't shake the feeling that there was more to this than he was letting on.

Taking a deep breath, Isolde stepped toward the throne, her heart pounding in her chest. The room seemed to hold its breath as she lowered herself onto the seat beside him.

And then, just as she settled, the flames in the hearth flared higher, casting a fiery glow across the room. A figure stepped forward from the shadows, draped in the blackest of cloaks, their face hidden beneath a veil of shadow.

Ryker's expression darkened.

"Someone else is watching," he muttered, his eyes narrowing. "And I fear they do not share our vision."

The air grew heavier, and for the first time, Isolde felt the full weight of the court pressing against her. The flames that had seemed so welcoming now felt like a threat. A danger she could not yet understand.

The court had many secrets.

And Isolde was about to uncover them all.

Two

Flames in the Snow

~~~~~~~~~~~~~~~~~~~~~~~~~~~~~~~~~~~~~~

Isolde woke to the smell of burning wood.

It wasn't the same scent that filled the Eternal Court's hearths. This smell was raw, acrid, different—like the scent of something long forgotten. It sliced through her dreams, pulling her from the warmth of the soft sheets into the biting cold of reality. The moment her eyes fluttered open, she knew something was wrong. The room was too still, too quiet. The heavy curtains that hung across the stone windows were drawn shut, but a strange, flickering light danced along the edges, casting shadows that writhed like dark creatures.

She sat up in bed, the motion slow and deliberate. Her fingers brushed the ornate sheets, but they felt strange, too heavy against her skin. She hadn't been asleep for long, but the fatigue in her bones made her feel as though she'd been here for an eternity. The warmth of the fire had been soothing, but now, it felt distant—like a memory she couldn't quite grasp.

And then, she heard it. A crackling sound, like the sound of something burning, but much more intense. More unnatural.

Isolde swung her legs off the bed and stood, her bare feet meeting the cold stone floor. The room was quiet again, save for the distant hiss of flame. But it wasn't a normal fire. The warmth in the room had evaporated, leaving her skin chilled as though she were standing in the heart of a storm. Her heart skipped a beat.

She moved toward the door of her chambers, her steps cautious, the soft sound of her footsteps swallowed by the thick silence of the court. Her hand hovered over the doorknob, hesitant. What could it be?

The crackling sound grew louder. It was as if the fire itself were reaching for her. A flash of bright light blazed from beneath the door, and the heat hit her like a wave. She flung the door open, not knowing what she'd find.

The sight before her stole her breath away.

Flames curled and twisted along the hallway, a roaring inferno that shouldn't have been possible. The stone walls were scorched, the air thick with the smell of burning wood and something darker—something that made her stomach churn. The fire didn't move like normal flames; it had a life of its own, seeping through the cracks of the palace as though it were alive, seeking something. Seeking her.

Isolde backed away, her heart hammering in her chest. The fire stretched toward her, but it didn't burn. It flickered, pulsed, and then it stopped, as if it were waiting.

Something was wrong. Something about this felt... unnatural.

A voice echoed through the corridor, low and filled with a chilling calm.

"Isolde."

She froze, every muscle in her body going rigid. Her breath caught in her throat, and the heat of the fire seemed to close in around her. The voice was unmistakable. Ryker. The Fire King. But this wasn't the warm, commanding tone she'd heard before. This was something darker, more insistent.

She turned toward the sound, her pulse quickening, and saw him standing at the far end of the hall. His silhouette was framed by the dancing flames, casting long shadows that stretched across the room. The fire flickered around him like a living thing, but he seemed unfazed, unaffected by the heat.

"Ryker," she whispered, her voice hoarse. Her heart raced with a mixture of confusion and fear. "What is this?"

His eyes—those molten amber eyes—gleamed with an unsettling intensity as he stepped closer, his footsteps silent against the stone. The fire seemed to follow him, curling around his feet like a serpent.

"This is a warning," he said softly, his voice colder than the winds of the Frostlands. "A warning you were meant to see. It is not a coincidence that you are here, Isolde."

She shook her head, her mind racing. "What do you mean?"

His eyes darkened, and the air around them seemed to thicken. "There are forces at play, forces that you don't understand. The court has its own agenda, Princess. And so do you."

His words struck her like a blow, but she stood her ground. "What do you want from me?"

Ryker's lips curled into a slight smile, but it didn't reach his eyes. "Nothing, yet everything."

The flames behind him roared to life again, their heat making the stone floor beneath her feet tremble. But it wasn't the flames that terrified her; it was the way Ryker spoke, as though he held the answers to everything she'd been searching for, and yet, offered none. There was something dangerous about the way he looked at her, as if he knew exactly what she was capable of—and what she wasn't.

She wanted to take a step back, to flee into the safety of her chambers, but she couldn't move. Her legs were frozen, her body unable to break free from the grip of his gaze. The flames flickered again, this time growing brighter, almost blinding. Her skin tingled, and the heat pressed against her chest, but she couldn't tear her eyes away from him.

"Why are you doing this?" she demanded, the words coming out more harshly than she intended. Her hands were clenched into fists at her sides, but the fire seemed to grow stronger with every breath she took, every word she uttered.

"I told you," Ryker said, his voice tinged with something that might have been amusement. "It is your destiny, Isolde. To join the fire and the frost. To choose one path or the other. And you will not escape that choice."

His words were like poison, sinking into her thoughts and twisting there, making her head spin. A deep dread took root in her chest as she realized the weight of what he was saying.

"You think I'm a part of your court, don't you?" she said slowly, her voice trembling despite her best efforts to remain steady. "But I'm not. I'm not one of you, Ryker. I don't belong here."

The smile that tugged at the corners of his lips faded, replaced by something darker, something ancient. "That is where you are wrong, Princess."

He took another step forward, the fire seeming to part for him, an invisible force pushing the flames back. His presence felt suffocating, the temperature around them rising to unbearable levels. She could feel the heat seeping into her skin, burning through her cloak and the layers beneath. But it was more than just physical discomfort. The fire felt like it was inside her now, crawling beneath her skin.

Isolde could feel her heart pounding in her chest, each beat louder than the last. She wanted to run, to get away from the oppressive presence that was Ryker, but the fire seemed to hold her in place, like it had chosen her. Like it had marked her.

"You are already bound to this court," Ryker whispered, his voice now a soft, dangerous promise. "And whether you like it or not, you will play your part in the coming storm."

The flames roared again, their heat unbearable, and for a moment, Isolde thought she might suffocate in the intensity of it all. But before she could react, the fire suddenly flickered, dying down, as if something—or someone—had intervened.

Ryker's eyes remained fixed on her. "Remember this moment, Isolde. The flames will always be with you. You can't escape them. Not now. Not ever."

And with that, he turned, his cloak billowing behind him as he walked away, leaving her standing alone in the corridor, the silence pressing in on her like a weight. The fire slowly faded, but its presence lingered, heavy and inescapable.

Isolde stood there, her breath coming in short gasps. The flames had come to warn her.

But there was no escape now.

Three

The Shattered Mirror

Isolde couldn't shake the feeling that something was wrong.

The fire had burned through the halls of the Eternal Court, an omen that seemed to follow her every step. No one in the court had spoken of it, but she knew they had all seen it. The flames that had curled in impossible patterns, reaching for her, seemed to linger in the air, a reminder that something far darker was at play than she had ever imagined. And yet, Ryker had said nothing more about it, leaving her to stew in the silence of her chambers.

Her mind churned with questions, her body restless. She could not understand what he had meant, what he had truly wanted from her. His cryptic words still echoed in her ears: You are already bound to this court, Princess.

Bound? To what? To him? To the fire?

She stood by the window now, looking out over the vast, sweeping landscape that stretched beyond the palace walls. Snow fell gently in the distance, but here, in the court, the air was thick with the warmth of the flames, the kind of heat that made her skin prickle with unease. She gripped the windowsill tightly, her knuckles white as she stared at the distant peaks of the Frostlands, a place that felt farther and farther away with each passing hour.

A soft knock on the door interrupted her thoughts.

"Enter," she called, her voice steady despite the storm of confusion inside her.

The door creaked open, revealing Elias, the court's enigmatic advisor. His dark cloak swept behind him, his long fingers curling around the doorframe as his sharp gaze fixed on her. He had the look of a man who carried a thousand secrets—secrets that were buried deep within the palace, locked away in rooms she could never reach. She had been wary of him from the moment they'd met, and the longer she stayed in the court, the more she felt that his presence was a constant reminder that things here were never as they seemed.

"Your Highness," Elias said, his voice smooth, almost too smooth. "The Fire King requests your presence in the grand hall."

A shiver ran down her spine at the mention of Ryker's name. His words from earlier that day resurfaced in her mind: *You are* already bound to this court. She had tried to push the thoughts away, but now, they came rushing back, unbidden.

"I'll be there shortly," Isolde replied, her voice betraying none of the unease that churned inside her.

Elias didn't move. Instead, he studied her for a long moment, his dark eyes narrowing slightly.

"There is something I must show you," he said, his voice soft but urgent. "Something that may help you understand the path that lies ahead."

Isolde frowned, unsure of what he meant. She had learned to distrust the man, to question his motives. He was never straightforward, always speaking in riddles and half-truths. But something in his eyes told her that she had little choice but to follow him now. The pull of the court was impossible to resist, and if there was something she needed to know, she had to trust that Elias would be the one to show her.

"What is it?" she asked, her tone cautious.

Elias stepped closer, his movements deliberate. "Follow me."

Without another word, he turned and walked down the hallway, his footsteps echoing against the stone walls. Isolde hesitated for only a moment before she followed, her heart pounding as she trailed behind him. The court was silent, save for the flickering flames that cast eerie shadows along the walls. The air grew warmer with every step she took, but it was the feeling of dread that pressed against her chest that made the temperature unbearable.

Elias led her to a door at the end of a narrow corridor, one that she had never noticed before. It was smaller than the other doors, its wooden frame intricately carved with symbols she couldn't understand. A strange hum seemed to emanate from the door, a vibration that pulsed through her bones.

"This is the room," Elias said, his voice low, as though he were afraid to speak too loudly in its presence. "What I am about to show you may change everything."

He reached for the handle and opened the door, revealing a dimly lit chamber. The air inside was heavy with the scent of old books and dust, but what caught Isolde's attention was the large, ornate mirror that stood against the far wall. It was unlike any mirror she had ever seen—its frame was made of blackened silver, twisted into shapes that seemed to writhe like flames. The glass, however, was what truly unsettled her. It didn't reflect her image as it should have. Instead, it was as though the glass held something else—something more.

Isolde stepped forward, her feet light on the cold stone floor. The mirror seemed to draw her in, its surface shimmering as if alive. She felt an inexplicable pull toward it, a force that made her breath catch in her throat.

"What is this?" she whispered, her voice trembling with a mix of awe and fear.

The Shattered Mirror

Elias didn't answer immediately. He stood behind her, watching her with an unreadable expression.

"The mirror reveals things that cannot be seen by the naked eye," he said at last. "It shows the truth beneath the surface, the things that lie hidden from you."

Isolde's fingers hovered above the surface of the glass. She could feel the heat radiating from it, as if it were alive, beating like a heart. Hesitantly, she placed her palm against the cool surface.

At first, nothing happened. The mirror's surface remained smooth and still, offering no indication that it was anything other than ordinary glass. But then, a faint glow began to pulse beneath the surface, like fire beneath ice. The image that appeared was not her own.

It was a reflection of the Eternal Court, but not the court she knew. This one was dark, its halls filled with shadows. The flames that had once danced in the hearths were now twisted, consuming everything in their path. She saw figures—figures she recognized—standing in the flames, their faces contorted in agony.

Isolde recoiled, her heart pounding in her chest. The mirror... it wasn't just showing her a reflection of the present. It was showing her something else. Something ancient.

"What is this?" she gasped, her voice barely a whisper.

Elias stepped closer, his expression unreadable. "This is the past, the future, and everything in between. This is the truth of the court, the truth you are bound to."

The reflection in the mirror shifted, revealing a different scene—a woman, draped in robes of ice, her face obscured by a crown of thorns. Her eyes glowed with an unnatural light, and her lips moved as though speaking in a language Isolde could not understand.

Isolde's breath caught in her throat. "Who is that?"

Elias's gaze hardened. "That is the one who came before you. The last heir of the Frostlands. The one who brought the flame and the ice together, only to tear them apart."

Isolde's heart skipped a beat. The last heir of the Frostlands? Was this woman her ancestor? Was she the one who had once been tied to the fire in the way Isolde was now?

The mirror flickered again, and the image shifted once more. This time, it was Ryker, standing alone in the heart of the palace, his eyes filled with sorrow and regret.

"She tried to stop it," Elias said quietly, as though speaking to himself. "But in the end, the fire consumes everything."

The reflection in the mirror shimmered, and before Isolde could take another step, the image vanished, leaving only the cold, still surface of the glass.

The Shattered Mirror

Isolde stood there, breathless, her mind reeling. The mirror had shown her the truth—the truth that no one had ever spoken of. The court, the fire, the frost—it was all bound together in ways she couldn't yet understand. And Ryker... the Fire King was hiding something. Something dark. Something dangerous.

"Why did you show me this?" Isolde asked, her voice a whisper of disbelief.

Elias's eyes narrowed as he stepped back. "Because it's time you knew. You are not just a pawn in this game, Isolde. You are part of something much larger. And the flames will never let you go."

The door slammed shut behind her, leaving her alone in the dimly lit corridor, her heart racing with the weight of the truth she had just seen.

Four

Beneath the Cinders

The air in the palace had changed.

Isolde could feel it the moment she stepped from her chambers into the grand hall, the weight of unseen eyes upon her. It was a suffocating feeling, as if the walls themselves were watching, listening, waiting for her to make her next move. She had tried to push the images from the mirror out of her mind, but they lingered like ghosts, haunting her every step.

She had seen the past—pieces of it, fragments that made no sense—and glimpses of what the future could hold, if the flames were allowed to consume everything. The ice and fire, the court, Ryker. It was all connected in ways she couldn't understand, and yet, it was undeniable. There was no escaping it now. She was bound to this place, whether she liked it or not.

Beneath the Cinders

But there was more. Elias's words, too, had left a lingering chill in her bones: You are part of something much larger. And the flames will never let you go.

As she walked down the marble corridor, the weight of those words pressed down on her chest, making it hard to breathe. She wasn't just a visitor in this court. She wasn't just a princess from the Frostlands. She was something more—something tied to the fire and the frost in ways that could burn her alive.

The sound of footsteps echoed through the corridor, sharp and sudden. Isolde turned, her heart skipping a beat, expecting to find Elias—or perhaps Ryker, his presence always heavy, always unsettling. But it wasn't either of them.

A figure stood at the far end of the hall, barely visible in the shadows. Their silhouette was cloaked in darkness, and the air around them seemed to ripple with an energy that made Isolde's skin prickle. She couldn't see their face, but she could feel their eyes on her, as if they had been watching her for far longer than she cared to admit.

"Who are you?" she demanded, her voice trembling despite her best efforts to remain calm.

The figure stepped forward, emerging from the shadows like a wraith. The cloak they wore shimmered with a faint, eerie glow, as if woven from the very light of the moon itself. When they spoke, their voice was low, almost a whisper, yet it carried an unmistakable authority.

"You've seen it, haven't you?" the figure asked. "The truth of the court."

Isolde's heart stuttered in her chest. She knew at once who this was, even though she had never seen their face before. This was the one who had been pulling the strings from the shadows, the one who had been orchestrating the court's movements, manipulating the flames and the ice alike. The advisor—the one who had been watching her all along.

"You're the one who—" Isolde began, but the words caught in her throat. She wasn't sure what she was going to say. How could she explain that she had seen the truth in the mirror, that the court was a lie? That Ryker was hiding something darker than she had ever imagined?

The figure's lips curled into a smile, and for a moment, Isolde could see the faintest glimmer of their face beneath the hood—a face that seemed too pale, too cold. Their eyes gleamed with something wicked, something ancient.

"Do not be afraid," they said, though their tone held no comfort. "You've seen what you needed to see. The fire, the frost, the destruction they bring. You are tied to it, Princess. Whether you accept it or not."

Isolde's breath hitched in her throat. This was what she had feared, what she had suspected. She had tried to deny it, tried to ignore it, but it was undeniable now. The mirror had shown her the truth—fragments of it, yes, but the truth nonetheless. The fire and the frost were two forces that could never coexist, and yet, she was caught in the middle of them.

She was the key.

She took a step back, her hands trembling. "What do you want from me?" she demanded, her voice steady but filled with barely contained panic. "What is it you want me to do?"

The figure tilted their head, the movement almost serpentine. "What do you think we want you to do, Princess?" Their voice was almost mocking, as though they found her confusion amusing. "We want you to choose. To choose the fire or the ice. The court or your people."

The walls around her seemed to close in, the air thick with the weight of their words. Isolde had always known this moment would come—the moment when she would have to decide, when the forces of fire and frost would demand her allegiance. But it had always felt like a distant future, something she could push aside. Now, it was here, and it felt like the weight of the world was on her shoulders.

"What if I don't choose?" she asked, her voice barely a whisper.

The figure's smile widened, and they stepped closer, their presence now overwhelming, suffocating. "Then the flames will consume everything, and there will be nothing left to save."

A chill crept down Isolde's spine, but it wasn't the cold that caused her to shiver. It was the certainty in the figure's words, the way they spoke as if they already knew the end of the story.

She turned, not willing to face them any longer. She needed to get away, to think, to breathe. But as she began to walk toward the grand hall, the figure's voice stopped her in her tracks.

"Remember, Princess," they called, their tone soft, like a promise. "The flames will always find you. And when they do, you will be the one to choose."

Isolde's heart raced as she walked away, her mind spinning with the weight of their words. The figure's words seemed to echo in her head, repeating over and over like a mantra. The flames would find her. But where would that leave her? What choice would she have?

She entered the grand hall, her steps quick and uneven, her heart pounding in her chest. Ryker stood at the far end of the room, his silhouette framed by the roaring fire that burned in the hearth. The flames flickered, casting eerie shadows across the room, and as Isolde stepped closer, she felt the heat of them, the pull of the fire, drawing her in.

But this time, she wasn't afraid of the fire. She was afraid of what lay behind it.

Ryker's gaze shifted to her as she entered, his amber eyes locking onto hers. There was something different in his expression this time—something harder, colder. But there was also an intensity, a fire in his eyes that made her skin prickle.

"Isolde," he said, his voice low and controlled. "You have seen the truth, haven't you?"

Beneath the Cinders

Her pulse quickened. "I don't know what you're talking about," she replied, her voice shaky, though she tried to sound more confident than she felt.

Ryker's lips curled into a smile, but it was a smile that didn't reach his eyes. "You don't need to lie to me. The flames always reveal what is hidden, whether we want them to or not."

The tension in the room thickened, the fire crackling ominously in the background. Isolde's heart raced as she met his gaze, her thoughts spinning. She had come here to pledge her allegiance, to accept her place in the court of fire and frost, but now—now she wasn't sure if she could trust anything she had been told.

The flames had shown her something. Something that was both a warning and a promise.

And she was beginning to wonder if she could survive the choice that was waiting for her.

The fire flickered in the hearth, casting long shadows that stretched across the room, wrapping themselves around her like a noose. Isolde took a step forward, but the weight of the decision hung in the air, thick and suffocating.

Ryker's eyes flickered to the flames, then back to her. "You will understand soon enough, Princess," he said, his voice soft and almost sad. "But by then, it may be too late."

The fire roared.

Five

Cold Hands, Warm Heart

The storm raged outside, its howling winds battering against the stone walls of the Eternal Court. Snowflakes danced in the air, swirling in a chaotic frenzy, but inside the palace, the warmth of the flames offered a false sense of safety. Isolde stood by the window, watching the storm's fury as it swept across the Frostlands, the winds howling with an eerie wail that sent a shiver down her spine.

She had learned to ignore the whispers that followed her through the halls, the murmurs of the courtiers who watched her every move. They knew she was different now—changed by the fire, by the mirror, by the strange figure who had warned her of the flames. She could feel it in the way they looked at her, as if she were something to be feared, something to be used.

But it wasn't their eyes she feared most. It was the ones that burned through her when she least expected it. Ryker's eyes, molten amber, watching her every moment. It was as though the fire inside him reached out to her, its pull undeniable, its warmth both comforting and suffocating. His presence lingered in every corner of the palace, a constant reminder that she was bound to this place, bound to him, whether she wanted to be or not.

The knock at her door startled her, breaking the silence of the room. She turned away from the window, her heart hammering in her chest, and walked toward the door.

"Enter," she called, her voice steady despite the sudden rush of unease that tightened her chest.

The door creaked open, and Elias stepped inside, his dark eyes scanning the room as though searching for something he couldn't find. His presence was always unsettling, like a shadow that never quite left her side, no matter how much she tried to escape it. He had been too quiet since the night of the mirror, his usual cryptic words replaced by an air of caution, as though he, too, were waiting for something—something neither of them could control.

"Your Highness," Elias said, his voice soft, yet filled with an underlying tension. "The Fire King requests your presence in the garden."

Isolde's pulse quickened at the mention of Ryker. The garden? It was the last place she wanted to be, alone with him, surrounded by the fire that had been clawing at her for days now. But she couldn't refuse. She was tied to this court, tied to its games and its secrets. The flames would find her, no matter where she went.

"Why the garden?" she asked, her voice barely above a whisper. "What could he possibly want from me there?"

Elias didn't answer immediately. Instead, he stepped closer, his gaze flickering toward the window where the storm raged outside. His lips curled into a faint, unsettling smile.

"It is a place of... reflection," he said at last, his tone almost playful. "Perhaps the Fire King thinks it's time for you to reflect on the choices before you."

The words hung in the air like a dark promise. The choices before you. Isolde could feel the weight of them pressing down on her, the walls of the palace closing in with every step she took toward the garden. The fire, the frost, the court—it was all a tangled web, and she was caught at the center of it.

"I'll go," she said, her voice firm. She had no choice. Ryker was waiting, and she could feel the heat of his presence even from across the palace. She had to face him, had to confront whatever it was he wanted from her.

As she followed Elias through the winding corridors, the air seemed to grow heavier, the scent of burning wood and incense mixing with the cold bite of the storm outside. The palace felt alive, its walls pulsing with an energy that made Isolde's skin crawl. She could hear the distant crackling of fire, the flickering flames that never seemed to die, no matter how many hours passed.

They reached the garden doors, and Elias paused, his hand resting on the handle.

"Be careful," he said softly, his voice laced with something unreadable. "The Fire King is not as he seems. Neither is the court. The flames are not just a force of destruction—they are a force of creation. And when they create, they can also destroy."

Isolde glanced at him, her brow furrowing in confusion. "What are you saying, Elias?"

But he was already gone, stepping back into the shadows as she pushed open the doors to the garden.

The moment she stepped outside, the heat hit her like a wave. The garden, once a serene haven of green and blossoms, now felt like a furnace. The flames of the Eternal Court licked at the edges of the space, creeping through the hedges and around the statues. The roses that had once bloomed in the garden were now scorched, their petals withered and blackened. The fire had taken over, consuming everything in its path, and there, in the center of it all, stood Ryker.

He was a silhouette against the roaring flames, his figure framed by the firelight, the heat radiating from him like a living thing. His amber eyes gleamed in the darkness, and when he spoke, his voice was both commanding and soft, as though the fire itself had seeped into his very soul.

The Eternal Court of Frost and Flame

"Isolde," he said, his tone low and inviting. "I've been waiting for you."

She didn't move toward him immediately. Instead, she stood there, her heart racing as she watched him. The fire that surrounded him seemed to pulse with life, its flames dancing in rhythm with the beating of her own heart. She could feel the warmth seeping into her skin, wrapping around her like a lover's touch, but it was the kind of warmth that burned, the kind that left scars.

"Why have you called me here?" she demanded, her voice steady despite the chaos inside her. She couldn't let him see how much he unnerved her, how much she feared what was happening between them.

Ryker stepped closer, his movements fluid, like the flames themselves. "I wanted to show you something," he said, his voice quiet but filled with an intensity that sent a shiver down her spine. "Something that may help you understand the choice you must make."

He reached out, his hand brushing against hers, and the heat of his touch spread through her like wildfire. Isolde's breath hitched as she fought to pull her hand away, but his grip tightened, his fingers cold as ice despite the heat that surrounded them.

"Isolde," he murmured, his voice barely above a whisper. "You are not just a princess. You are something more. Something both of the frost and the flame. And if you choose to accept it, you will have the power to change everything."

She pulled her hand from his grasp, the fire around her flickering and dimming, but only for a moment. "I don't want your power," she said, her voice sharp. "I didn't come here for that."

Ryker's lips curled into a smile, though there was no warmth in it. "You think you have a choice in this, but you don't. The fire will claim you, whether you accept it or not. It is already inside you."

Isolde took a step back, her mind whirling with his words. The flames, the frost, the power he spoke of—it was all a trap. A trap she couldn't escape, no matter how hard she tried.

The air around them seemed to crackle with tension, the flames growing higher, hotter, as though they were responding to the storm inside her. The fire was beckoning her, its pull undeniable, but something within her—something deep and ancient—told her that accepting it would mean losing herself.

She was caught between the two forces, the fire and the ice, each one pulling her in different directions. And Ryker—Ryker was the key to it all. He was the one who held the flames in his hands, and he was the one who could either burn her alive or offer her the salvation she so desperately needed.

"I don't want to be your pawn," she said, her voice shaking but strong.

Ryker's smile faded, his expression hardening as the fire around them flared higher. "You already are, Isolde. You always have been."

The flames roared louder, drowning out her thoughts, and for a moment, she was lost in the heat, in the fire that seemed to consume everything.

But she couldn't stay here. She couldn't let him control her, not anymore.

With a final, defiant glance at him, Isolde turned and ran. The fire chased her, its flames licking at her heels, but she refused to look back. The heat burned her skin, but she wouldn't let it burn her soul.

Not yet.

Six

The Inferno's Song

T he darkness of the Eternal Court had never felt so suffocating.

Isolde paced through the palace halls, her mind a whirlwind of confusion, fear, and anger. The flames still burned in the garden, their intensity now a distant memory, but the heat lingered in her skin, in the pit of her stomach. She had felt it when she ran—felt the fire chase her, never relenting, always just behind her. And even now, hours after she had locked herself in her chambers, she could still feel its presence, pressing against her, crawling beneath her skin.

She had tried to push the image of Ryker out of her mind—the fire that burned in his eyes, the way he had touched her, the way he had spoken to her as though he knew everything about her, as though she were nothing more than a pawn in his game. She had run from him, but she had learned that running wouldn't help. It never did. The fire was a part of her now, as much as the frost.

A faint, almost musical sound drifted through the air, pulling her from her thoughts. It was a soft melody, eerie and hypnotic, like a lullaby that twisted the soul. It seemed to come from nowhere, echoing through the palace like a ghost's song. The sound was so haunting, so beautiful, that it sent a shiver down Isolde's spine.

She stood still, her breath catching in her throat. What was this?

The melody grew louder, swirling around her, wrapping itself around her mind. It wasn't just a song—it was a call. A summons. The fire had always spoken to her, but this… this felt different. This felt like a command.

She moved toward the source of the sound, her feet moving of their own accord. Each step felt like it took her deeper into the heart of the palace, deeper into the unknown. The song pulled at her, urging her forward, and she could not resist. It was as if the very walls of the court were alive, their secrets reaching out to her, drawing her in.

The halls grew colder as she moved, the flickering torches casting long shadows on the stone walls. The fire that had once surrounded her now felt distant, replaced by a strange chill that gnawed at her bones. The further she went, the darker the palace became, the more oppressive the silence grew. The melody was now louder, louder than anything she had ever heard, reverberating through her very soul.

Isolde stopped in front of a door she had never seen before. It was made of dark wood, intricately carved with symbols she didn't recognize—runes that seemed to shift and move beneath her gaze. The song came from behind it, calling her, beckoning her to open the door.

Her hand trembled as she reached for the handle, but before she could touch it, a voice echoed from the darkness.

"Do not open that door."

Isolde froze, her heart thudding in her chest. She knew that voice. It was Elias.

He stepped from the shadows, his dark eyes flashing with warning, but there was something else in his gaze—something deeper, more urgent.

"Elias," Isolde whispered, her voice barely audible. "What is this? What's behind this door?"

Elias's gaze shifted to the door, his face paling as if he were seeing something that made him uneasy, something that threatened him. His fingers twitched at his sides, but he did not move to stop her. He merely stood there, as though paralyzed by something that held him back.

"You don't understand," Elias said, his voice low and strained.

"That song is not what it seems. It's an invitation—an invitation you cannot accept."

Isolde's mind raced. The song. The door. Everything about this moment felt wrong, but it also felt inevitable. The fire, the frost—it was all pushing her toward this moment, this door. She could feel it in her very bones, the pull of something ancient, something dangerous.

"What is behind this door, Elias?" she demanded, her voice shaking with frustration. "Why won't you tell me?"

Elias's expression softened for a brief moment, and he stepped closer, his voice low and urgent. "You don't know what you're dealing with. That song—it's not just a melody. It's the voice of the Eternal Flame itself. The one that has been imprisoned for centuries. If you open that door, you will awaken something that should never be freed."

Isolde's heart skipped a beat. The Eternal Flame. The name sent a chill through her, a terror that she couldn't explain. She had always known that the flames had power, unimaginable power, but this—the Eternal Flame—was something else. Something ancient, something that could destroy everything.

"You mean the fire... it's alive?" Isolde whispered, her voice trembling.

Elias nodded, his face grim. "More than alive. The Eternal Flame is the source of all fire in the court, the heart of the kingdom. It is bound by magic, by a power that can only be

The Inferno's Song

controlled by one who is both fire and frost. And that is you, Isolde. You are the key to unlocking its power."

Isolde stepped back, her breath catching in her throat. She had known, deep down, that she was tied to something greater than herself. The fire, the frost, the palace—it all circled around her, as if she were the center of a force beyond her understanding. But this? This was something else entirely.

Elias continued, his voice urgent. "If you open that door, you will unleash the power of the Eternal Flame. And once it is free, there will be no stopping it. The world will burn, and the frost will be consumed. Everything will be reduced to ash."

The song grew louder, more insistent, and Isolde could feel the heat rising in her chest, the fire within her stirring. It was as if the flames were waking, calling her to them. The temptation to open the door, to step into the fire, was overwhelming, but she couldn't. She couldn't let herself be consumed by it.

"What do I do?" she asked, her voice barely a whisper.

Elias's eyes flickered with something—perhaps regret, perhaps fear—as he stepped closer, his presence a quiet, haunting weight. "You must resist, Isolde. The song will try to pull you in, but you must fight it. If you give in, there will be no turning back."

For a moment, Isolde was still, the weight of his words settling over her like a shroud. The door beckoned, the song wrapped around her like a lover's embrace, but Elias's warning was clear. *If you give in, there will be no turning back.*

But the flames inside her stirred again, whispering promises of power, of control, of freedom. They wanted her to open the door. They wanted her to free them. And yet, she knew deep down that if she did, she would lose herself, consumed by the fire, lost to its insatiable hunger.

She took a deep breath, forcing herself to step back, away from the door. "I won't open it," she said, her voice firm despite the chaos inside her.

For a moment, the song seemed to pause, the silence deafening in the stillness of the hall. But then, the flames around them flickered, and the pressure in the air seemed to increase, as if the court itself were holding its breath, waiting for her next move.

Elias's eyes softened, a flicker of something like relief passing over his face. "You made the right choice," he said softly. "But remember, Isolde—the flames will never stop calling you. You are their heir, and they will always seek to claim you."

Isolde's heart pounded in her chest as she turned away from the door. The fire would always be there, just out of reach, calling to her, pulling her in. But for now, she had resisted. For now, she had made her choice.

The storm outside raged on, but Isolde could feel the heat inside her, the fire that would never fade.

Seven

A Kiss of Flame

Isolde stood at the edge of the palace's grand balcony, staring out into the vast expanse of the kingdom below. The storm that had ravaged the Frostlands had finally subsided, leaving behind a landscape blanketed in soft white snow. The winds had died down, and the night air felt crisp and fresh, as though the world had been cleansed. But the peace outside was at odds with the turmoil inside her.

She could still feel the echo of the Eternal Flame's song, pulsing in her veins, in her heart. It had been days since she had resisted the urge to open that door, but the pull of the fire had not faded. It whispered to her in the quiet moments, when the palace was still, when she could hear nothing but her own breath and the rhythm of her heartbeat. The fire had claimed a part of her, and she wasn't sure if she would ever be free of it.

The warmth in her chest seemed to flare, a flicker of flame, and she instinctively placed her hand over her heart, as though she could smother it. But the heat only grew. It was a hunger, a desire that gnawed at her from the inside out, urging her to give in, to let the flames consume her.

The doors behind her creaked open, but Isolde didn't turn around. She already knew who it was. The air in the room shifted, the familiar heat of his presence filling the space. Ryker. The Fire King.

"Isolde," he said, his voice soft, yet full of a tension that seemed to vibrate in the air. "I've been looking for you."

She closed her eyes, letting the sound of his voice wash over her. The fire inside her stirred in response, like a restless beast awakening from a long slumber. The connection between them was undeniable, and it was growing stronger with each passing day. Every time he spoke her name, every time their paths crossed, it was as though the flames that lived within them both burned brighter, hotter, until they were consumed by the same fire.

"I'm here," she said, her voice a mixture of defiance and reluctance. "What do you want from me, Ryker?"

There was a pause, a moment of silence that felt heavier than any words he could say. Then, slowly, Ryker approached, his footsteps light but deliberate, as though he were moving closer to something precious, something fragile.

"I want nothing more than to help you understand," he said, his voice low, almost a whisper. "To help you see what is waiting for you."

Isolde turned then, her heart racing as she faced him. He was standing only a few steps away, his molten amber eyes locked on hers. The fire that surrounded him seemed to pulse with life, reaching toward her, as though it, too, were drawn to her presence. She could feel the heat emanating from him, like the sun on a summer day, warming her skin, seeping into her bones.

But there was something else in his eyes—something darker, something that unsettled her. The flames flickered in his gaze, but there was a storm beneath them. A storm that threatened to consume everything in its path.

"Understand what?" Isolde asked, her voice barely a whisper. Her heart pounded in her chest as she took a step back, trying to put some distance between them. But Ryker moved forward, closing the gap between them with a single stride.

"This," he said, his voice thick with intensity. He reached for her, his hand brushing against her cheek. The touch was gentle, but the heat that radiated from his skin was anything but. It burned her, searing through the fabric of her gown, through the layers of protection she had built around herself. "This is what you were always meant to be. The fire and the frost, together. And together, we can make it all burn."

His words struck her like a blow, leaving her breathless. She felt the heat rise in her chest again, spreading through her like wildfire. It was as though his touch had awakened something deep inside her, something primal, something that wanted to give in, to let the flames consume her.

She closed her eyes, fighting the pull. "I don't want this, Ryker. I don't want to be part of your court, part of your fire."

The heat in his gaze flared, and for a moment, Isolde thought she saw a flicker of something—something like pain—in his eyes. But it was gone in an instant, replaced by the familiar intensity that always seemed to surround him.

"You don't have a choice, Isolde," he said softly, his voice almost tender. "The flames have already chosen you. And I—" He paused, his breath catching for a moment. "I've already chosen you, too."

Before she could react, Ryker leaned in, his face inches from hers, his breath warm against her skin. Isolde's heart raced in her chest, her body betraying her as the flames within her stirred, reaching for him. She wanted to pull away, to stop him, but the pull of the fire, the pull of him, was too strong.

And then, his lips were on hers.

The kiss was fiery, urgent, as though the flames had taken on a life of their own. It was a kiss that burned, a kiss that seared through her, leaving a trail of heat in its wake. Isolde's breath hitched as the fire inside her roared to life, as if it had been waiting for this moment, this connection. It was a connection she had resisted for so long, but now that it was here, she couldn't deny it.

She felt the heat of his body against hers, the warmth of the fire seeping into her very soul, and she knew, without a doubt, that this was no ordinary kiss. This was a kiss of flame, a kiss that would leave its mark on her forever.

But it wasn't just the fire. As their lips parted, Isolde could feel the frost inside her stirring, too, as though it were awakening in response to the fire. The two forces—fire and ice—were battling within her, pushing and pulling, both of them fighting for control.

She pulled away from him, her chest heaving with the effort, and looked into his eyes. "What are you doing to me?" she whispered, her voice trembling with a mixture of confusion and desire.

Ryker's gaze softened, and for the briefest moment, the intensity faded. "I'm not doing anything to you, Isolde," he said, his voice low and almost sad. "I'm just showing you what's always been inside you. The fire and the frost, bound together. You can't escape it. Neither of us can."

Isolde's mind raced as she tried to make sense of his words, of the fire that still burned in her chest, still roared in her veins. She had resisted it for so long, but now, now it felt like a part of her—like a truth she couldn't escape.

"I don't want to be a pawn in your game, Ryker," she said, her voice steady despite the storm of emotions inside her. "I want to choose my own path."

"You can't choose, Isolde," Ryker said, his voice soft but filled with an edge of finality. "The path has already chosen you."

The flames flickered around them, as though they were listening to his words, as though they, too, were waiting for her to understand. Isolde's heart pounded in her chest, and she realized, with a sinking feeling, that there was no escaping it. The fire and the frost. They were a part of her now, and there was nothing she could do to change that.

Ryker stepped back, his eyes never leaving hers. "The fire will always be with you," he said softly. "But it will be your choice whether to let it consume you or use it to burn the world."

Isolde's mind was spinning, her body still tingling from the kiss, from the fire that had been awakened inside her. She knew one thing for certain—the path she had been walking was no longer her own. And the flames would lead her, whether she was ready or not.

As she looked into Ryker's eyes, she understood: The fire was never just about him. It was about her. And she could feel it in her soul—that she was already lost to it.

Eight

Echoes of the Past

The wind howled through the open window, its cold breath curling around Isolde as she sat by the fire. She stared into the flickering flames, mesmerized by their dance. Each movement seemed to whisper her name, the heat from the hearth licking at her skin, reminding her of the kiss that had ignited the fire within her—the same fire that continued to burn, deep in her chest, every second of every day.

It wasn't just the fire, though. The ice, too, had awakened inside her, its cold tendrils wrapping around her heart, numbing the fear that had once gripped her. The two forces, fire and frost, were no longer separate. They were one, inseparable, bound together by something far more powerful than she could ever have imagined.

She closed her eyes, trying to push away the images that had plagued her since that moment—since the moment when Ryker had kissed her, sealing her fate. Her mind raced with confusion, her thoughts twisting like the flames in the hearth. What was she supposed to do? Where could she go? The palace had become a prison, its walls closing in around her, and the fire—always the fire—was just beyond her reach, beckoning her to let it consume her.

But she couldn't let that happen. Not yet.

A sudden crash broke through her thoughts, a sound that echoed through the silent halls of the palace. Her heart skipped a beat, her body instantly on alert. She stood up, her pulse quickening, her senses sharpened. She moved toward the door, hesitating for only a moment before she swung it open.

The hallway was dim, the flickering torches casting long shadows that seemed to stretch and writhe in the gloom. Isolde's breath caught in her throat as she noticed the bloodstained footprints leading down the corridor. The blood was fresh, the scent sharp in the air, and she couldn't shake the feeling that it was a warning.

Her heart raced as she followed the trail, her footsteps echoing in the eerie silence. The palace felt colder now, as though the very walls were closing in around her, urging her forward. She turned a corner and froze.

The sight before her made her blood run cold.

A figure lay on the floor, motionless, their body twisted in an

Echoes of the Past

unnatural way. Blood pooled around them, staining the stone floor, and Isolde's stomach churned at the sight. She recognized the figure immediately—it was one of the guards, a man she had seen countless times before in the halls of the palace. But now, he was nothing more than a lifeless body, his face contorted in an expression of terror.

Isolde knelt beside him, her hands trembling as she touched his cold skin. There was no pulse. He was gone.

The sound of footsteps behind her made her jump, and she turned quickly, her heart pounding in her chest. Elias stood in the doorway, his dark eyes wide with alarm.

"Isolde, you shouldn't be here," he said, his voice strained.

She didn't answer immediately. She couldn't. Her mind was spinning with questions, with fear. Who had done this? Why?

Elias's gaze shifted to the body on the floor, his face tightening. "There's no time for this," he said, his voice harsh. "You need to come with me. Now."

Isolde stood up, her body stiff with tension. She opened her mouth to protest, but Elias didn't give her the chance. His hand shot out, grabbing her arm with surprising force.

"Come," he repeated, his voice quieter now, but urgent. "You don't understand. There are things happening in this court, things you don't know about. We need to leave."

Isolde jerked her arm away, shaking her head. "Leave? What are you talking about? Who did this?"

Elias looked around nervously, his expression shifting from concern to something darker, something unreadable. "You need to understand, Isolde. There's more at play here than you realize. The court... the fire... they've been hiding the truth from you."

The fire. The word hit her like a punch to the stomach. She had felt it before—the flames, the heat, the pull—but now, it felt different. It was as though the fire had been watching her all along, waiting for the right moment to reveal its true nature.

She stepped back from Elias, her body tense. "What do you mean? What truth?"

Elias hesitated, his eyes darting around the hallway as though he feared someone might be listening. "There are forces in this court that have been manipulating everything—the fire, the ice, the throne. Ryker... he's not who you think he is."

Isolde's heart skipped a beat. She felt the blood drain from her face, her head spinning with confusion. "What are you talking about? Ryker's the Fire King. He's... he's the one who's been guiding me."

Elias's eyes darkened. "Guiding you? Or controlling you?" He stepped closer, lowering his voice to a whisper. "Ryker is the key, Isolde. He's been using you, just like the rest of them. The flames are not just a force of nature—they are a prison. And

Echoes of the Past

you, you are the key to unlocking it."

The words hit her like a thunderclap, and for a moment, she couldn't breathe. The fire was a prison? Had she been living in a lie all this time?

She shook her head, unable to accept it. "No. I don't believe you. Ryker—"

"Ryker is cursed," Elias interrupted, his voice sharp. "He is bound to the fire. And so are you, now. But there's more. There are those in the court who have been waiting for this moment—waiting for you to break free of the fire's control."

Isolde's breath came in shallow gasps as she struggled to process what Elias was saying. The fire had been calling to her, that much was clear. But now, the idea that it was a prison, a curse—it shattered everything she had believed.

She looked at Elias, her heart hammering in her chest. "What do I do?" she whispered, her voice cracking.

"You have to come with me," Elias said, his tone softening. "I can help you, Isolde. I can show you how to break free."

Before she could respond, the palace shook, a tremor running through the stone walls that rattled the windows and sent a shiver down her spine. The ground beneath her feet seemed to vibrate, the air growing thick with an oppressive pressure. Isolde's heart raced as the lights in the hallway flickered and went out, plunging them into darkness.

A low, guttural roar echoed from somewhere deep within the palace, reverberating through the halls. The sound was deafening, filling her chest with an unshakable fear. It was the fire. She could feel it, pulsing with a malevolent force, alive, awakening.

"This is it," Elias said, his voice grim. "The flames are rising. You have to choose, Isolde. Now."

Before she could respond, the doors at the end of the hallway burst open with a violent crash. Figures in dark cloaks flooded the room, their faces hidden, but their presence unmistakable. The flames flickered in their wake, casting long shadows that seemed to stretch toward her, pulling her in.

Elias stepped between her and the newcomers, his face hard with determination. "Stay behind me," he whispered.

But it was too late.

The fire surged forward, its heat rising, and Isolde felt herself being drawn toward it, her body betraying her, her thoughts clouded by the flames that consumed her soul. She tried to resist, to fight it, but the fire was too strong.

She had always known that the flames would come for her. But now, standing in the heart of the court, she understood: The flames had never been hers to control. They were only waiting for the moment when she would finally break.

Nine

The Phoenix's Flame

The air was thick with the scent of burning wood. The palace, once a sanctuary, now felt like a furnace, its heat pressing against Isolde's skin, tightening her chest. The flames crackled and roared, but they were no longer the familiar warmth she had come to associate with the Fire King. No, this was something else—a force far darker, far more ancient.

Isolde stood at the threshold of the throne room, her heart pounding in her chest. The heavy doors loomed before her, dark and foreboding, their edges flickering with the same unnatural fire that had consumed the halls of the palace. The flames danced around her feet, a constant reminder of the power she was tied to—power that was now slipping beyond her control.

She had resisted it for so long, fought the pull with every ounce of strength she had. But now, standing here, with the flames at her feet, she understood something she hadn't before. The fire wasn't just a part of her. It was her. It had always been there, waiting to claim her, to burn through her veins like wildfire.

The tremor in the ground beneath her feet was growing stronger, and the roar of the flames intensified, filling her ears with a deafening sound. She stepped forward, her breath shallow, her body moving on its own as the fire beckoned. There was no turning back now.

With a deep breath, Isolde pushed the doors open.

Inside, the room was shrouded in darkness, but the flickering light of the fire cast long shadows across the walls, stretching like tendrils of smoke. The Phoenix's flame, she realized, was not just an element of fire—it was something far greater. Its warmth filled the air like a living thing, wrapping itself around her, pressing against her like an invisible hand.

At the center of the room, on the throne, sat Ryker.

His figure was bathed in the golden glow of the flames, his eyes glowing with the intensity of the fire, as if the very flames of the Phoenix were bound to him. He looked almost otherworldly, his form shadowed and surreal, as though he were no longer fully human. His presence filled the room with a magnetic force, drawing her in, and she could feel the fire reaching for her, pulling her toward him.

"You've come," Ryker said, his voice low and filled with an

unspoken promise. "I knew you would."

Isolde didn't respond immediately. Instead, she took a step closer, the fire seeming to part for her, as if it recognized her. The flames licked at her feet, but she didn't feel their burn—not anymore. The warmth was in her now, a part of her, coursing through her with every beat of her heart.

"You don't have to do this, Ryker," she said, her voice shaking despite her best efforts to remain steady. "This power—it's consuming us. It's consuming everything."

Ryker's gaze hardened, and he stood, his movements slow and deliberate, as if he were savoring the moment. The flames around him flared with life, rising higher, their heat intensifying as he stepped forward.

"It's not consuming us," he said, his voice barely above a whisper. "It's freeing us. This power—it's not just the fire. It's the Phoenix. And you, Isolde, are its heir. You were always meant to be."

She shook her head, stepping back, but the flames seemed to follow her, their heat pressing against her skin like a suffocating weight.

"No," she said, her voice stronger now, more resolute. "I don't want this. I didn't ask for this."

Ryker's expression softened, just for a moment, before his eyes burned brighter, filled with something darker, more dangerous. "But you don't get to choose anymore. The Phoenix has chosen you. The flames—this power—it's in your blood. And now, you have a choice: embrace it, or let it consume you."

Isolde's heart hammered in her chest as the flames began to swirl around her, their movement erratic, as though they were alive, their hunger insatiable. She could feel the pull—the desire to give in, to let the fire engulf her, to become one with it. The temptation was overwhelming, but she fought against it, gritting her teeth, focusing on the voice in her mind that whispered of ice, of control, of the strength she had within her to resist.

"No," she whispered again, more fiercely this time. "I will not become this. I will not become the Phoenix's slave."

A low laugh rumbled from Ryker's chest, and the flames around him flared, casting shadows across the room. "You already are, Isolde. You just don't realize it yet. The fire will burn through you. It will burn away the ice that holds you back, the fear, the doubt."

The flames surged, growing higher, their heat unbearable now, but Isolde stood her ground. She could feel the power coursing through her, the fire and ice battling within her, both forces warring for dominance. The Phoenix's flame was too strong, too ancient to ignore.

She clenched her fists, her nails digging into her palms as she fought against the pull. She had to stay strong. She had to resist. But the flames—they were everywhere, inside her, around her, urging her to give in.

The Phoenix's Flame

"You cannot escape what you are," Ryker said, his voice now a low, almost seductive murmur. "The Phoenix will rise within you, and you will be its vessel. Together, we will remake the world."

Isolde felt the fire surge in her chest, threatening to break free, and for a moment, she thought she might lose herself to it, might let the flames consume her entirely. But then, just as the heat reached its peak, something inside her snapped.

No.

She pushed the fire back, focusing on the coldness within her—the ice that had always been there, that had always anchored her. The ice was her strength, her clarity. The fire might burn, might call to her, but she would not let it swallow her whole. Not again.

With a sharp breath, she extended her hand, the ice within her rising to meet the flames. The two forces collided in an explosion of heat and cold, the air crackling with the energy of the clash. The Phoenix's flame roared, but the ice held strong, surrounding it, controlling it, pushing back against the fire's insatiable hunger.

Ryker stepped back, his eyes wide with surprise as the flames around him began to shrink, to flicker and die, unable to compete with the force of the ice that was now enveloping them both.

"You think you can control it?" Ryker sneered, his voice

dripping with disbelief. "You think you can control the Phoenix?"

Isolde's heart raced, but she held firm, the ice spreading from her fingertips, encasing her in a shield, wrapping around the flames that sought to engulf her. "I will control it," she said, her voice steady despite the chaos around her. "I will control the fire."

The flames crackled and snapped, but the ice held them at bay, pushing them back, forcing them to bend to her will. For a brief moment, there was silence, a stillness that filled the room, as though the world itself was holding its breath.

And then, with a final surge of power, Isolde willed the fire into submission. The Phoenix's flame flickered, its heat diminishing, until only a faint glow remained, pulsing weakly in the air before finally dying out.

Isolde stood there, breathing heavily, her heart racing in her chest. The fire was still there, deep within her, but she had beaten it back. She had taken control. For now.

She turned to Ryker, who stood in stunned silence, his gaze fixed on her. His face was a mask of fury, of disbelief, but beneath it—beneath the rage—there was something else.

Fear.

"You may have won this battle, Isolde," he said, his voice low and dangerous. "But the Phoenix will rise again. And when it does, you won't be able to stop it."

Isolde's heart pounded in her chest, but she didn't flinch. She knew what he was saying was true—the Phoenix's flame could not be extinguished forever. It would rise again. But next time, she would be ready.

"I'll be ready," she said, her voice steady.

Ryker's eyes darkened, and for a brief moment, Isolde saw the full weight of the fire in them, the burning desire for control, for power. But then, just as quickly, it was gone, replaced by something colder, something more calculating.

"You've made a mistake, Isolde," he said, his tone venomous. "You've made an enemy of the wrong force."

And with that, he turned and walked away, the flames fading with his departure.

Isolde stood alone in the throne room, her body trembling with exhaustion, but her resolve stronger than ever. The battle had just begun. And she would fight—not just for herself, but for the world that was about to burn.

Ten

The Icebound Secret

The night air was cold enough to cut through to the bone.

Isolde stood in the shadow of the old watchtower, her breath a visible cloud in the dim light of the moon. The wind howled around her, the blizzard that had begun hours ago now turning into a full-fledged storm. Snowflakes fell thick and heavy, swirling in the gusts, but they barely touched her skin. The ice that clung to the stone walls of the watchtower seemed to mock her—reminding her that the cold, no matter how much she fought it, was always close, always within reach.

She had come here for a reason. The palace was no longer safe. Ryker's hold on her had grown stronger, the fire inside her a constant, gnawing presence. Every step she took felt like she was walking on the edge of a cliff, the pull of the flames

The Icebound Secret

threatening to drag her over. But there was something else—something deeper—that gnawed at her.

The ice.

The ice had always been a part of her, but it had never felt so distant. She had kept it buried, pushing it aside as the fire surged within her, but now... now it felt like a whisper in the back of her mind, a reminder of the control she had lost. The fire and the ice—two opposing forces, each one battling for dominance within her.

But that was not what had brought her here tonight.

A door creaked open behind her, and Isolde stiffened. She didn't need to turn around to know who it was. His presence was as unmistakable as the fire that burned in his veins. Elias.

"Isolde," he called, his voice soft but urgent. "You shouldn't be out here in this storm. It's not safe."

She didn't respond immediately, her gaze still fixed on the tower before her. There was a chill in the air that wasn't just the cold. It was the silence. The kind of silence that made her feel as though something, or someone, was watching her. The wind seemed to carry an echo with it, a distant sound of something breaking, something crumbling. Her heart raced.

"I need to be alone, Elias," she finally said, her voice steady, but tinged with an underlying edge of desperation. "I need to understand what's happening. Why the ice is calling me. Why I can't control it."

Elias stepped closer, his boots crunching softly in the snow, but he didn't press her. His figure was obscured by the blizzard, but the warmth he carried with him—his calm, steady presence—was enough to make the air feel a little less oppressive. She could feel the weight of his gaze, the concern, the understanding, but also something darker beneath it. He knew more than he was telling her.

"The fire is strong," Elias said softly, his voice cutting through the howl of the wind. "But the ice—it's not something to ignore. You've always known it was there, Isolde. Now, it's time to understand why."

Isolde turned to face him then, her breath visible in the freezing air. "Why now, Elias? Why is it that every time I try to understand, the fire takes over? Why can't I feel the ice the way I used to?"

Elias didn't answer immediately. Instead, he glanced around, his eyes narrowing slightly. There was a tension in the air that made her uneasy, as if they were being watched.

"You've been walking in the fire's shadow for too long," he said, his voice low, almost too low. "The flames have clouded your judgment. They've drowned out the truth you've been hiding from."

"The truth?" Isolde asked, her voice rising with the sudden weight of suspicion. "What truth?"

Elias stepped closer, his face tense, his eyes filled with an emotion she couldn't read. "The ice is not just a part of you. It's a key. A key to something much larger. Something you were meant to unlock."

"Unlock?" Isolde echoed, confused and more than a little wary. "Unlock what?"

Elias glanced around once more, and for the first time, she saw the flicker of something like fear cross his face. He reached out, grabbing her arm with surprising force.

"Come with me," he urged, his voice frantic now. "It's time you understood what you are—what you're meant to do."

Before Isolde could protest, Elias pulled her through the snow, his grip tight on her arm. The wind seemed to shift as they moved, becoming harsher, as if the storm itself were conspiring against them.

They crossed the outer courtyard and moved toward a set of ancient stone stairs that led to a forgotten part of the palace—an area long sealed off, hidden from the rest of the court. Isolde's pulse quickened, and she felt an unsettling sense of foreboding.

"What is this place?" she asked, her voice trembling as they descended into the darkness.

"It's where the truth is buried," Elias replied, his tone grim. "The truth about your bloodline, about the ice and the fire. It's all here."

They reached the bottom of the stairs, and the air grew colder still. The stone walls of the underground chamber seemed to pulse with a life of their own, the shadows shifting in ways that made Isolde's skin crawl. A single torch flickered weakly on the far wall, casting an eerie glow over the room.

Elias walked toward a large, carved door at the far end of the chamber, its surface covered in intricate runes. Isolde could feel the pull of the door even before Elias touched it. The air seemed to crackle with energy, a hum that vibrated in the very air around her.

"Isolde," Elias said, his voice barely a whisper. "Behind this door lies the secret you've been running from. The truth of your power."

She hesitated, her hand resting on the cold stone as she gazed at the door. A strange feeling washed over her—a mix of fear, curiosity, and the undeniable sense that whatever was behind this door could change everything. The ice inside her stirred again, this time more violently than before.

"I can't do this," she whispered, stepping back.

"You can," Elias said, his voice urgent. "You must. This is the only way to gain control over the fire and the ice. You've always known this was your destiny."

Isolde swallowed hard. Her fingers brushed the door, and with a soft creak, it opened, revealing a hidden chamber bathed in shadow.

The Icebound Secret

At the center of the room was a pedestal, and atop it, encased in ice, lay something that took Isolde's breath away. It was a crystal—clear, glowing with an ethereal light, pulsing softly as if it were alive. The air around it shimmered, and she could feel the intense power emanating from it, the same power that had been calling her for so long.

Elias stepped beside her, his voice low. "This is the Heart of Ice. The source of all that you are. And the key to your freedom."

Isolde's hand hovered above the crystal, but she hesitated. "What do I do with it?"

"You must claim it," Elias replied, his eyes dark with something she couldn't place. "You must become one with it. Only then can you control the fire and the ice. Only then can you end the cycle of destruction that's been set in motion."

Isolde's breath caught in her throat. She could feel the fire inside her, rising, growing restless, as though it was aware of what was about to happen. The ice, too, responded, its chill now sharp, biting at her skin. The two forces clashed within her, fighting for control, but the Heart of Ice seemed to hold a power beyond either.

With a deep breath, Isolde reached for the crystal.

The moment her fingers touched the cold surface, a jolt of energy shot through her. The room around her seemed to explode in light, and for a moment, she couldn't breathe, couldn't move. The fire inside her flared, the ice surged, and all at once, the two forces collided with an intensity that felt like the world was coming undone.

The heart of ice pulsed, and Isolde felt herself falling into the depths of the crystal, the world around her spinning into a whirlwind of fire and frost. The truth was closer now, closer than ever before.

But the question remained—would she survive the truth that lay within her?

Eleven

The Awakening Flame

~~~

T he world shattered.

Isolde's breath caught in her throat as the Heart of Ice pulsed once again, its energy flooding through her in waves that seemed to tear apart the very fabric of her being. Her senses were overwhelmed—fire and ice clashing violently within her, surging in ways that defied comprehension. Her body felt as though it was being torn in two, both forces tugging at her soul, each one demanding dominance.

Her vision blurred, the room spinning wildly around her. The stone walls of the hidden chamber warped and twisted, dissolving into nothingness as though they were being swallowed by the very flames and frost that fought for control inside her. The crystal's glow intensified, casting shadows that danced like living creatures, and the blinding light enveloped her entirely.

For a brief, fleeting moment, she thought she might die—consumed by the very powers that had once been her allies and her enemies. But then, as the chaos swirled around her, the world stopped.

Silence.

A heavy, suffocating silence filled her ears, and the world returned to its place. The storm outside—the howling wind, the swirling snow—was gone. The chamber, the pedestal, and the Heart of Ice were still there. But now, everything felt... different. There was an unnatural stillness in the air, a weight that pressed down on her chest.

Isolde opened her eyes slowly, her head heavy with exhaustion. The light from the crystal had faded, but something inside her still burned—a deep, unwavering fire that pulsed in time with her heartbeat. Her body, too, was no longer hers to command. She could feel the ice within her, but it no longer felt like an opposing force. It felt like something else, something familiar, something she could almost reach out and touch.

"You've done it," Elias's voice broke through the silence, his words barely above a whisper, filled with awe.

She turned to face him, her limbs stiff as if she had been frozen for years. He was standing in the doorway of the chamber, watching her with an expression she couldn't read—eyes wide, his posture tense.

"What... what happened?" she asked, her voice hoarse. Her

throat felt like sandpaper, raw and cracked, as though she had screamed for hours, though she didn't remember doing so.

Elias's gaze flickered to the Heart of Ice, now dim and still on its pedestal, as if it had returned to its slumber. He took a step closer, his brow furrowed. "You've unlocked it," he said, his voice tight. "The true power that lies within you. The Heart of Ice is now bound to you—part of you."

Isolde's chest tightened. She could feel the weight of his words, the implications of them settling in her bones. She looked down at her hands, which trembled slightly, still tingling with the remnants of the energy that had coursed through her moments ago. The fire that had once raged inside her—wild, uncontrollable—was now tempered, the coldness of the ice wrapping around it like a barrier.

But it wasn't just that. The fire had changed, too. She could feel it now, hot and steady, as if it were no longer a force to be feared but something to be wielded. The two opposing forces had finally fused together inside her. And though they no longer fought for dominance, the power they gave her was a double-edged sword.

"You're wrong," she whispered, barely able to form the words. "I don't feel like myself anymore."

Elias stepped closer, his hand hovering near her shoulder, but he stopped himself before touching her. "You never were just yourself, Isolde. Not in the way you thought. You were always meant to be both. The fire and the ice are in your blood. You've just unlocked the part of you that had been hidden, buried for so long."

Isolde closed her eyes, trying to push away the overwhelming weight of the truth. She had always known she was different, but now... now it felt like she was something else entirely. The fire burned hot within her, but the ice kept it in check, a constant battle between passion and control. And deep down, she knew that it was only a matter of time before one of them—one of her—would rise above the other.

A low rumble echoed through the chamber, causing the stone walls to tremble. The sound was distant at first, but as it grew louder, Isolde's blood ran cold. It was the kind of rumble that signaled the approach of something massive—something powerful. The flames inside her flickered in response, and the ice rose, but she couldn't shake the feeling that whatever was coming was more than she could handle.

Elias looked up sharply, his face a mask of concern. "It's starting," he muttered, barely audible. "The fire is awakening. You've unlocked its true power, but with it comes a force you're not ready for."

"What is it?" Isolde asked, panic creeping into her voice.

The walls seemed to close in, the temperature in the chamber rising to an unbearable degree. The fire inside her roared in response, surging outward, as though it, too, could sense the threat. Elias's expression darkened.

"You've given the fire access to the Phoenix's flame," he said, his voice filled with dread. "And once it awakens, nothing will be able to stop it."

The floor beneath them rumbled again, this time more violently. The walls of the chamber cracked, and pieces of stone began to fall, littering the ground around them. The flames inside Isolde flared uncontrollably, the power she had just gained now threatening to rip her apart. She reached out, her hand instinctively raising to try and steady herself, but the force of the power within her was too much. The room seemed to shift around her, the walls growing darker, the air thickening with heat and pressure.

"Isolde, you need to fight it!" Elias shouted, his voice strained. "You need to control it! If you let the fire take over, it will consume everything. You will become nothing more than a weapon—a force of destruction."

Isolde closed her eyes, her chest rising and falling with each panicked breath. The flames were everywhere—inside her, around her, in the very air she breathed. The Phoenix's flame had awoken, and with it, a power she wasn't prepared for. She could feel it pushing against her, demanding release, threatening to break free.

No.

She couldn't let it consume her—not again. She had to hold on, to keep control, or else everything she had fought for would be lost. The fire and the ice, together, had given her strength, but she had to be the one to wield it.

She reached deep inside herself, searching for the part of her that could fight back. The ice that had always been her anchor, the part of her that had kept her from falling into the flames, was still there. It was faint, but it was there.

With a forceful breath, she drew on that cold, that control. The ice surged within her, pushing back against the fire, not to extinguish it, but to temper it. Slowly, painfully, the flames began to recede, the heat subsiding, the room growing quieter.

The rumbling stopped, the stone walls halting their tremors. Isolde's chest heaved with the effort it had taken to contain the power, but she could feel the balance returning. She wasn't fully in control yet, but for the first time, she felt the possibility of it.

Elias's gaze softened, though there was still a trace of worry in his eyes. "You did it," he said, his voice quiet with awe. "You've controlled it—for now."

Isolde took a shaky step forward, her hand still trembling at her side. She could still feel the fire, still feel the ice, but now they were… tempered. Balanced. But she knew, deep down, that balance was fragile. The forces inside her could rise again, could break free at any moment.

But for now, she had won. And that, in itself, was a victory.

"I don't know how much longer I can keep this under control," she said, her voice hoarse but determined. "The fire—it's too strong."

Elias nodded, his face grim. "For now, you have control. But the Phoenix's flame… it's a part of you now. And it will never be completely contained. You'll have to learn to live with it. Learn to wield it, or it will destroy you."

Isolde didn't answer. She couldn't. The battle was far from over. But for the first time since she had unlocked the ice and the fire within her, she felt a glimmer of hope. If she could control this power—if she could learn to wield it—perhaps there was a way to stop the destruction.

The storm outside raged on, but inside the chamber, Isolde stood tall, her heart steady, her resolve unbroken. The flames may burn, but they would not consume her.

Not today.

Twelve

The Burning Veil

───❦───

The palace had never felt so alive, and yet so dead at the same time.

Isolde stood in the heart of the grand hall, her fingers trembling at her sides, the air heavy with the promise of something darker, something inevitable. The flames burned low in the hearths, casting flickering shadows against the cold stone walls, but their warmth did little to soothe the chill that had settled deep inside her. She could still feel the pull of the Phoenix's flame, lingering just beneath her skin, like a sleeping beast waiting to awaken.

The fire had become part of her, inseparable from her essence, and yet, the more she struggled to control it, the more it seemed to slip beyond her grasp. The ice inside her, once a source of strength, now felt like a distant memory. The balance she had

The Burning Veil

fought for was fragile, like glass, and each day it seemed to crack a little more.

Her eyes scanned the room, drawn to the intricate tapestries that hung on the walls, their colors now muted in the dim light. The once grand hall, filled with laughter and light, now felt suffocating, as though the very air was thick with the weight of something terrible about to unfold.

A movement in the corner of her vision made her freeze. Ryker stepped into the room, his presence so overwhelming that it was as if the flames themselves were drawn to him. His silhouette was framed by the archway, his amber eyes glowing with an intensity that sent a shiver down her spine. The heat from his presence seemed to fill the room, pressing against her skin like a physical force.

Isolde's heart stuttered, but she refused to show any weakness. She straightened her back, raising her chin in defiance, but deep inside, she could feel the fire inside her stir, a response to him that she could no longer control.

"Ryker," she said, her voice steady despite the tension that tightened around her chest. "What are you doing here?"

His lips curled into a smile, though it didn't reach his eyes. He stepped closer, each step measured, his gaze never leaving hers. The flames in the hearth seemed to grow brighter, reflecting the fire that burned in him.

"You've been avoiding me, Isolde," he said, his voice smooth, almost coaxing. "I don't appreciate being ignored."

"I'm not ignoring you," she said, her hands clenched into fists at her sides. "I'm trying to understand what's happening to me. To this place. To us."

Ryker stopped just in front of her, his eyes never leaving hers. He was so close now that she could feel the heat radiating from him, and it made her skin burn, as if she were standing too close to a flame. The fire in him—the Phoenix's flame—was so strong, so undeniable, that it almost suffocated her.

"You're fighting it," he said, his voice barely a whisper. "Fighting what we both know is inevitable."

"I'm not fighting anything," Isolde snapped. "I'm trying to stay sane, trying to keep control before everything goes up in flames."

Ryker chuckled darkly, his breath warm against her ear as he leaned in closer. "You don't understand, do you? You think you're in control, but the flames have already claimed you. I've already claimed you."

Isolde recoiled, her pulse racing as the flames inside her surged in response to his words. She had known, deep down, that this was always where it would lead. The fire, the ice, and Ryker— they were all tied to her in ways that she couldn't escape.

"I won't be your pawn, Ryker," she said, her voice shaking, but her resolve unbroken. "I won't let you use me for your own gain."

His gaze softened for a moment, almost as if he were truly considering her words. But then, without warning, he reached out, his hand brushing against her arm, sending a jolt of heat through her skin. The fire inside her flared, responding to him like a beast awakened from a long slumber.

"You're not a pawn, Isolde," he said, his voice softer now, though still filled with an edge of command. "You're the queen. The one who will reign over both the fire and the frost. You just don't realize it yet."

A strange, almost aching sensation settled in her chest as his words sank in. Queen. The thought was both terrifying and intoxicating. She had always known that there was something greater inside her, but the power that he was offering—the throne—was more than she could bear. It was a weight she wasn't sure she was ready to carry.

"I don't want to rule over destruction," she whispered, the words slipping from her mouth before she could stop them. "I don't want to be a part of your kingdom of fire."

Ryker's expression darkened, and the temperature in the room seemed to drop, the fire flickering in the hearth. "You have no choice, Isolde," he said, his voice low, filled with a raw intensity that made the air crackle. "The throne is yours, whether you accept it or not. The Phoenix's flame is yours, and it will rise. You can't hide from it."

Isolde took a step back, her heart racing in her chest. The fire was rising inside her again, the heat becoming unbearable. She could feel it—the pull of the Phoenix, the desire to give in, to let it consume her and become one with the flames.

But she couldn't. Not like this. Not if it meant losing herself completely to Ryker's will.

"I will fight it," she said, her voice steady, though her legs trembled beneath her. "I will fight you."

Ryker's eyes flashed with something darker—something that sent a shiver down her spine. For a brief moment, she saw the full weight of the power he controlled. The Phoenix's flame was not just a force of nature—it was a force of destruction, capable of ripping through everything she had ever known.

"You can't fight it, Isolde," he said, his voice cold, final. "The fire is inside you now. You are the Phoenix. And you will burn."

Before she could react, Ryker stepped away, his presence retreating as quickly as it had come. But the heat he left behind lingered, the fire still burning within her, demanding to be freed.

The flames in the hearth flickered once more, their light growing dimmer as the tension in the room stretched taut. The silence that followed felt suffocating, as if the very walls of the palace were holding their breath.

Isolde turned away, her chest heaving with the weight of the

The Burning Veil

encounter. She could feel the fire and the ice inside her, each one vying for control, each one threatening to tear her apart. She wasn't sure how much longer she could hold on.

But she had to. She had to keep fighting. Because if she didn't, she would become nothing more than a puppet—an instrument of destruction in Ryker's hands.

And she wouldn't let that happen.

Not now. Not ever.

The palace felt more oppressive than ever as she walked through the halls, her heart pounding with every step. The fire would burn, yes—but she would not let it consume her.

Not yet.

Thirteen

The Ashes of Betrayal

The corridors of the palace were deathly silent, the only sound the soft click of Isolde's boots against the cold stone floors. The air had grown heavier since her confrontation with Ryker. The flames that had once felt like an ally were now more like a curse, burning hotter every time she thought of him. She could still feel his words echoing in her mind, the promise of the Phoenix's flame, the threat of what she would become.

Betrayal.

The word was a weight on her chest, suffocating her with its meaning. Ryker had shown her his truth, a truth twisted with power and control, but it was not the only truth in this palace. There were secrets here, buried deep, and for the first time, Isolde realized that the very foundation of the court might be a lie. She had to know the truth. She had to find the answers, even if they meant facing the darkness inside herself.

She moved through the halls with purpose, but her mind was scattered. The flames pulsed beneath her skin, reaching for her, beckoning her to give in. The ice, once so steady and reassuring, now felt distant, as if it too was slipping away from her grasp. She had always been strong, always held on to control, but now, after everything that had happened, she wasn't sure if she was still the same person.

As she reached the end of the hallway, she stopped. There was a door there, one she had never seen before, hidden behind a tapestry. The wood was old, its surface worn with age, and the carvings that adorned it were intricate and familiar. The patterns spoke of power—of something ancient. A strange feeling crept up her spine as she reached for the handle. She could feel the heat radiating from the wood, but beneath it, the coolness of the stone seeped through, reminding her of the ice that still lingered inside.

She hesitated for only a moment before she opened the door.

Inside was a chamber bathed in shadows, the flickering light from the corridor barely illuminating the room. The air was thick with dust, and the scent of old parchment filled her nose. Bookshelves lined the walls, their contents stacked in disarray, as though someone had rifled through them in a hurry. In the far corner, a large table was covered with maps and documents, and a strange, ancient artifact stood in the center—a blackened crystal, glowing faintly in the dim light.

Isolde stepped forward, drawn to the artifact. The crystal seemed to hum with energy, its pulse in sync with the fire inside her. She reached out, her fingers brushing against its surface. The moment her skin made contact, a jolt of power shot through her, a surge of heat that coursed through her veins like wildfire.

The room shifted, and for a moment, she felt as though the walls were closing in on her. The fire, the ice—everything seemed to fade away, replaced by a vision, a glimpse into the past.

A vision of the court.

The scene before her was haunting, like a memory that wasn't hers. She saw herself—another version of herself—standing in the middle of the grand hall, her eyes wild, her hands glowing with the same fire that surged through her now. She was surrounded by shadows—figures she didn't recognize—whispers of betrayal curling through the air.

"You have to choose, Isolde."

The words echoed in her mind, and she gasped, stumbling back from the crystal. The vision faded, but the cold feeling of dread remained. Her chest tightened as the truth began to settle in. The power, the fire—she wasn't the first to be bound by it. And whatever had happened here, whatever had been hidden in the depths of the palace, was far darker than she had ever imagined.

Suddenly, she heard the softest sound—a creaking, like the weight of footsteps on the old wooden floor. She spun around, her heart pounding in her chest, but the room was empty.

Isolde didn't have time to think. She turned and ran toward the door, her breath quickening as she raced back into the hallway. The vision had unsettled her, but there was something else—a feeling that had been gnawing at her since she entered this place. She couldn't shake the sense that someone else knew the truth. Someone else had been watching her.

She was about to turn the corner when she collided with someone. The impact sent her stumbling backward, her hand reaching for the wall to steady herself.

"Careful," a voice said, low and smooth, as the figure before her steadied her with a hand on her arm.

Isolde's pulse surged as she looked up into the eyes of the last person she wanted to see.

Ryker.

His gaze softened as he took a step back, but there was something about the way he looked at her—something calculating, something hungry. The heat that radiated from him burned through her, and she instinctively pulled away, her fingers trembling at her sides.

"What are you doing here?" she demanded, her voice sharp with a mixture of anger and fear.

Ryker's lips curled into a smile that didn't reach his eyes. "I could ask you the same question."

Isolde's chest tightened as she glanced around the corridor, as if the walls themselves were closing in. She had to get away from him. She had to understand what she had seen, what was buried in this palace. But she couldn't let Ryker see the fear rising inside her. She couldn't let him know that she was beginning to doubt everything she had believed.

"I'm here to find the truth," she said, her voice trembling despite her best efforts. "The truth about this place. About you."

Ryker's smile faded, and for a brief moment, his eyes darkened with something unreadable. "You don't want to find the truth, Isolde. Not if you knew what it really meant."

"What do you mean?" she asked, her heart racing as the heat from the flames inside her flared. She couldn't stop herself from reaching for the power that burned within her. It was as though the fire was alive, responding to the tension between them.

Ryker took a step closer, his presence overwhelming, the air around them charged with electricity. "The truth is a dangerous thing. Some things are better left hidden."

Isolde's breath caught in her throat as he reached out, his hand brushing against her cheek with a tenderness that made her skin burn. The flames surged in response, but she held them back, desperate not to let him control her. Not again.

"I'm not afraid of the truth, Ryker," she said, her voice shaking but defiant. "I'm not afraid of you."

The Ashes of Betrayal

Ryker's eyes narrowed as he stepped back, the warmth of his presence lingering in the space between them. The tension in the air grew unbearable, and for a moment, neither of them moved. The flames and ice inside her roared in response to the pull between them, each force threatening to break free.

"You will be," he said softly, his voice filled with a quiet, dangerous promise. "You'll learn that the truth always burns."

And with that, he turned and walked away, leaving Isolde standing in the hallway, her heart pounding in her chest. She could feel the fire inside her—the hunger, the power—raging against her control, but she couldn't let it take over. Not yet.

She had to find the answers. She had to uncover the truth.

But as Ryker's footsteps faded into the distance, Isolde knew one thing for certain: the truth would burn her, too.

She just didn't know how long she could survive the flames.

Fourteen

The Flame and the Frost

Isolde's mind raced as she walked down the winding corridors of the palace. The fire within her pulsed with every step, like a heartbeat of its own, its heat sinking deeper into her skin. The icy grip of the frost seemed distant now, as if it had retreated, leaving her vulnerable to the flames. Ryker's words echoed in her ears, and with each passing moment, they gnawed at her resolve.

"You will be… consumed by the flames."

She had tried to block out the memories, to push away the way the fire had wrapped around her soul when he touched her, the way the heat from his body had surged into her like a spark catching dry wood. The power, the control—it was undeniable.

But with it came the danger. The hunger.

The Flame and the Frost

She stopped in front of a large, ornate door, its edges worn with time, yet still imposing. The palace's forgotten wing. The place she had been drawn to earlier, the room with the strange artifact—the Heart of Ice. The same door she had found herself standing in front of so many times, a door she never dared open. Until now.

Tonight, everything felt different. She couldn't explain it, but something in the air, in the very stone beneath her feet, felt charged—like the calm before a storm. The walls seemed to pulse, as if breathing, the stone faintly warm, then cold, as though the pulse of the palace was tied to her every move.

Isolde pushed the door open.

The room was quiet. Too quiet.

Dust motes floated lazily in the dim light, undisturbed by any breeze. The Heart of Ice was still resting on its pedestal, the crystal glowing faintly, as if aware of her presence. But it wasn't the artifact that held her attention. It was the figure standing in the corner of the room, their face hidden beneath a hood.

The temperature dropped sharply, the chill seeping into her bones, and for a moment, she couldn't breathe. The ice. It was here, in full force, and it recognized her.

"Isolde," a voice rasped, barely audible over the crackle of the faint fire in the hearth. The tone was cold, far colder than the frost she had come to understand. The kind of cold that froze you from the inside out.

Her heart skipped a beat as the figure stepped forward into the light, their eyes gleaming from the depths of their hood. They were tall, their presence imposing, like a shadow cast by the moon itself.

"Who are you?" Isolde demanded, stepping back instinctively, her fingers twitching, ready to call upon the flames inside her. She could feel the fire stirring, threatening to surge to the surface, but she fought to keep it at bay.

The figure didn't answer immediately. Instead, they tilted their head, their lips curling into a smile that was more chilling than reassuring. "Ah, so it's true," they said softly, as though speaking to themselves. "The ice and the fire, together at last. How interesting."

Isolde's pulse quickened. The words felt wrong, unsettling in ways she couldn't explain. How could they know about the fire? The frost? Her?

"What do you know about me?" she demanded, her voice steady, but there was a tremor beneath it.

The figure's smile widened, though there was nothing kind in their expression. "Everything. You've been chosen, Isolde. Chosen to wield both the fire and the frost. But like everything else in this cursed court, there are consequences to such power."

Her chest tightened. "What consequences?"

The figure stepped closer, and though their features were still hidden, there was an unmistakable air of authority about them. They had the voice of someone who had been in control, who had seen things no one else could understand.

"The flames have been awakened," the figure said, their voice low, almost a whisper, "but they can only burn so long before they consume everything. And when the fire is no longer enough, the ice will come, spreading through everything it touches. It will turn the world to nothing but snow and cold."

Isolde's breath caught in her throat. The ice. The fire. Everything was connected to her now, and the weight of it—the responsibility, the power—was suffocating.

"No," she whispered, shaking her head. "I won't let that happen. I won't let it consume me. I can control it."

The figure laughed softly, a sound that sent a shiver through her. "Control? You think you can control what is inside you? The ice and fire are not meant to be controlled. They are meant to be used. And when you fail to use them, they will destroy you. And everyone around you."

Isolde felt the weight of their words settle deep within her. The fire and the frost, once a part of her, now felt like chains, pulling her toward something darker. Something she had never intended.

"Who are you?" she asked again, her voice demanding an answer, though fear twisted inside her. "What do you want with me?"

The figure took another step closer, their cold gaze never leaving hers. "I am someone who has seen the consequences of awakening the Phoenix's flame. Someone who understands what it can do when it burns unchecked. I came here to help you, Isolde. But you're not ready. None of you are."

Isolde took a step back, her heart racing. "What do you mean? What happened to the others? What happened to the first?"

The figure's smile faltered, just for a moment. "The first? The one who thought they could wield both powers? They were nothing but a fool. They couldn't control the fire. They couldn't survive the frost. And in the end, they were consumed by both."

Her pulse quickened as the realization hit her. The figure was talking about herself—the last person who had tried to wield the Phoenix's flame, the one whose failure had been buried in the past. And now, here she stood, just as broken, just as vulnerable, with the same power coursing through her veins.

"No," Isolde whispered, shaking her head, trying to block the vision that swirled in her mind. "I won't be like them. I won't let this destroy me."

The figure reached up, pulling back their hood, revealing their face. Isolde froze. The face was familiar—a face she had seen only in the distant memories of those who had lived before her. A face that had been erased from history. A ghost.

"You are them," the figure said, their voice hard. "The one who failed. The one who was supposed to bring balance. But now, you are nothing but a tool—a weapon. And soon, you will burn just like the rest."

Isolde's breath caught as she stepped backward, feeling as though the very walls of the chamber were closing in on her. The fire inside her surged, but she could feel the ice threatening to rise as well. She couldn't breathe.

"No!" she cried out, the flames erupting from her palms, their heat spilling into the room. But the figure didn't flinch. They were unmoving, unfazed by the fire that roared around them.

"You cannot escape your fate, Isolde," the figure said softly, their tone full of sorrow. "The flame and the frost will claim you. And nothing you do can change that."

Isolde's vision blurred, her thoughts scattered as the fire and the frost fought for dominance. The figure's words echoed in her mind, their meaning sinking in with terrifying clarity. The choice had never been hers. The power had always been too much, too strong, and now, it was too late.

The fire burned.

The frost froze.

And Isolde was caught in the middle.

The walls around her seemed to tremble, the sound of ice cracking and fire roaring filling her ears. She couldn't escape it. There was no way out.

But she would not give in. Not yet.

Not while she still had a choice.

Fifteen

The Final Ember

The storm had returned.

Outside the walls of the palace, the wind howled with a fury that rattled the very stones. Snow swirled through the air in thick, white sheets, obscuring everything beyond the courtyard. But inside, the atmosphere was even more oppressive, the air heavy with the tension that had been building for days. Isolde could feel it in every step she took, every breath she drew. The fire and the frost inside her were at war, their battle now undeniable, their clash echoing through her soul.

She stood at the edge of the grand hall, staring at the empty throne. The seat that had once been a symbol of power and authority now seemed like a mocking reminder of the choices she had yet to make. The fire inside her burned hotter than ever, the flames threatening to consume everything in their path, while the ice chilled her heart, holding her in place, preventing her from making a decision. The two forces within her fought for control, but neither was willing to yield.

"You're here," a voice broke through the silence, and Isolde spun around, her pulse quickening as she saw Ryker stepping from the shadows. His presence was as imposing as ever, the warmth of his body almost palpable, filling the room with the heat of his power.

Isolde's heart beat faster, the fire responding to him instantly, but she pushed it back, forcing herself to stand still. "What do you want, Ryker?" she asked, her voice steady, though she could feel the fear creeping into her chest. "What more is there to say?"

Ryker smiled, though it was cold, devoid of any warmth. "There's always more to say, Isolde. You've known this was coming. You've always known that we were meant to rule together."

"I don't want to rule with you," she snapped, her fists clenching at her sides. "I don't want any part of your kingdom, your fire. I'm not your queen."

Ryker's eyes glinted with something dark, something dangerous, as he took a step closer. "You don't get to choose, Isolde," he said softly. "The fire has chosen you. And when it burns, it burns everything in its path. There's no escaping it."

Isolde felt the fire flare within her, the heat rising, but she fought against it. She had spent too long resisting, too long holding back. The fire was her enemy now, as much as it had once been her ally. "I won't let it burn me," she said, her voice cold with defiance. "I won't let it burn this world."

"Then you'll have to fight for it," Ryker said, his voice suddenly serious, the playful edge gone. He stepped even closer, his presence overwhelming. "But you won't win, Isolde. Not unless you learn to embrace the fire. You can't fight it forever."

"I don't want to embrace it," she spat, her anger flaring. "I don't want to become a weapon, a force of destruction."

"You already are," Ryker replied, his voice like ice. "You've always been. The fire, the frost—they are both part of you. You can't fight them. Not anymore."

The words hit her like a blow. She had always known the fire was inside her, but she had never understood how deeply it had embedded itself in her soul. And the ice—she had thought the cold was her strength, her control, but now it felt like a prison. The two forces inside her were tearing her apart, and she wasn't sure how much longer she could hold on.

"I won't be a puppet for you," she said through gritted teeth. "I won't let you control me."

Ryker's gaze softened, but the darkness in his eyes was still there, lurking beneath the surface. "You think you have control, Isolde," he said softly, almost sympathetically. "But the fire has always controlled you. It's always been in you. And when it awakens, there's no stopping it."

Isolde's hands trembled at her sides as the heat surged through her, the flames burning hotter, faster, like they were alive, feeding on her fear, her anger, her pain. She could feel it now—how the fire had always been with her, how it had always controlled her. She had never truly been free.

"Then what?" she asked, her voice breaking. "What do you want me to do? Give in? Let the flames consume me?"

Ryker stepped closer, his eyes locking onto hers, his voice low and dangerous. "Yes. Let it consume you. Let the fire take what it wants, and you'll be free. You'll be the queen of the ashes, the ruler of the Phoenix's flame."

For a moment, Isolde felt the heat rise again, the pull of the fire so strong, so overwhelming that it almost felt like she was drowning. The flames surged inside her, the ice retreating, melting away, leaving her vulnerable to the fire's power. She could feel it, could taste it, could sense the destruction it would bring.

But deep down, she knew she couldn't give in. The flames would consume everything, everything she loved, everything she had fought for. She couldn't let it destroy her.

"No," she whispered, her voice steady despite the storm raging inside her. "I won't give in. I won't be your queen. Not like this."

The Final Ember

Ryker's smile faded, and the temperature in the room seemed to drop. The fire that had filled the room now flickered, its light dimming as though it were retreating from her. For a moment, the silence between them was thick, suffocating.

"You think you can stop it?" Ryker asked, his voice low, almost a growl. "You think you can hold back the flames?"

Isolde stood tall, her chest rising and falling with each breath. The fire inside her was still there, still raging, but she held it at bay, keeping it from consuming her. The ice, too, was within her, waiting for its moment. She had learned to control both forces, to balance them, and she wasn't going to let Ryker take that from her.

"Yes," she said, her voice unwavering. "I can stop it. I will stop it."

Ryker stared at her for a long moment, his expression unreadable. Then, with a sharp exhale, he turned away, his cloak billowing as he walked toward the door.

"Then we'll see," he said, his voice cold. "We'll see if you can control it. If you can survive the flames."

Isolde stood there, her heart pounding, the fire and ice still raging inside her, but for the first time, she felt something else—a sense of clarity. She didn't have to give in to the flames. She didn't have to let them consume her. She could fight. She could win.

She would.

As the door slammed behind Ryker, the room was left in silence. The fire still burned, but it was no longer in control. Isolde had taken the first step toward mastering it, toward claiming her own fate. The battle wasn't over, but she knew one thing for certain:

She was not going to let the flames burn her.

Not yet. Not ever.

www.ingramcontent.com/pod-product-compliance
Lightning Source LLC
LaVergne TN
LVHW020425080526
838202LV00055B/5039